9.40

A Family in the Persian Gulf

This book takes you on a trip to Bahrain, in the Persian Gulf. There you will meet the Al-Alrifi family. Ahmed Al-Alrifi is an artist and he will show you some of his work. Kawkab, his wife, will tell you all about the religious customs of her country. You will learn about what the family like to eat and what their hobbies and interests are.

FAMILIES AROUND THE WORLD

A FAMILY IN
THE PERSIAN GULF

Peter Otto Jacobsen
Preben Sejer Kristensen

The Bookwright Press
New York · 1985

Families Around the World

First published in the United States in 1985 by
The Bookwright Press
387 Park Avenue South
New York, NY 10016

First published in 1985 by
Wayland (Publishers) Limited
49 Lansdowne Place, Hove
East Sussex BN3 1HF, England
© Copyright 1985
Text and photographs
Peter Otto Jacobsen and
Preben Sejer Kristensen
© Copyright 1985 English-language edition
Wayland (Publishers) Limited

ISBN 0–531–18003–4
Library of Congress Catalog Card Number: 84–73579

Printed by G. Canale and C.S.p.A., Turin, Italy

Contents

Flying to the Persian Gulf

We are flying to the Persian Gulf to visit a family who live in Bahrain. As we approach our destination we see below us the vivid blue waters off the coast of Iran and the barren desert of the Qatar peninsula. This area is dotted with spectacular flares of waste gas burning in the oilfields.

Gas flares – a waste of a precious resource.

Bahrain – its name means "two seas" – consists of an archipelago of thirty islands and is one of eight countries which lie on the Persian Gulf. The others are Kuwait, Saudi Arabia, Qatar, the United Arab Emirates, Oman, Iran and Iraq. All of these countries have become rich since the discovery, this century, of their oil resources.

Bahrain is more important as an exporter of refined petroleum than as a producer. Most of the crude oil for refining is pumped from Saudi Arabia in an underwater pipeline.

The Persian Gulf is the stretch of water between the Arabian peninsula and Iran. It is the most important source of oil and gas in the world.

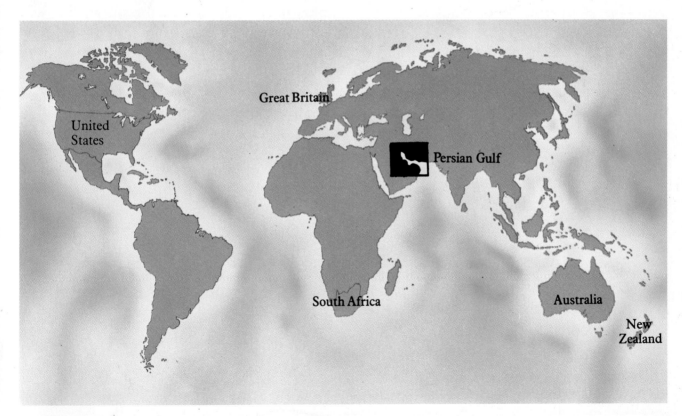

Landing in Bahrain

We land at the airport on Muharraq Island, which is the main international airport for the state of Bahrain. It is quite near the capital, but on a neighboring island to the northeast. We get into a chauffeur-driven car at the air terminal, sent by the Ministry of Information, and head for Manama, the capital. Leaving behind the bustling port of Muharraq, we cross the causeway to Bahrain Island.

We are driven speedily into Manama, along the beautiful coastline, to our luxury hotel. The streets here are wide and lined with trees. Among the people jostling together, we can see women dressed completely in black. They are also wearing veils so only their eyes can be seen. This reminds us that we are in an Islamic country, where the women traditionally wear such clothing.

Islam is the main religion throughout the Middle East. It is based on the teachings of the prophet Mohammed. He was a member of a semi-nomadic people who lived in the seventh century. It is believed

Manama, the capital of Bahrain, lies in the north of the island. It is a very modern city.

that the Angel Gabriel appeared to him several times. In these visions Mohammed was instructed to go and preach the word of God.

We arrive at the hotel and step out of our air-conditioned car into the intense heat. The temperature in this part of the world rarely falls below 29°C (85°F) for six months of the year!

Bahrain is the smallest country on the Persian Gulf, with an area of 669.26 sq. km. (260 sq. mi.)

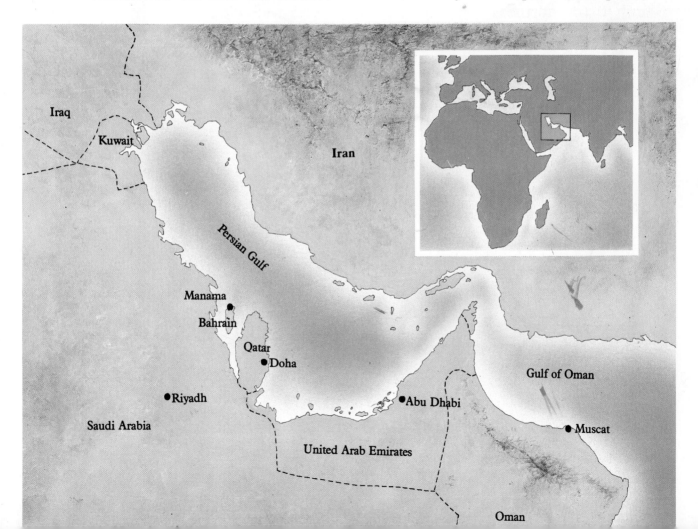

Exploring Manama

A crowded street in the souq *in Manama.*

We are spending the night in Manama before going on to Isa Town, about 8 kilometers away, where we will meet the Al-Alrifi family. Isa Town is one of the new towns built for Bahraini citizens. The land was donated by the Emir Al-Khalifa, the ruler of Bahrain. It was designed to provide modern housing for 15,000 people.

We have plenty of time on our hands so we decide to go and explore the town. From the central square we walk down to the *souq*, or bazaar. You can find these in many Middle Eastern cities. We wander along the narrow streets which are full of stores selling almost everything you could want – fruit and vegetables, televisions, kitchen equipment, clothing, spices, perfumes and much more. As we walk further into the *souq* the streets become narrower and narrower. Turning right we walk into a very busy street with stores overflowing with gold trinkets, necklaces, rings, earrings and bracelets. Jewelry still makes up an important part of the traditional gift from a husband to his new bride.

A veiled woman does her household shopping in the souq.

The *souq* is very near the mosque. The mosque is the Muslim place of worship and is often domed and beautifully decorated. Ahmed Al-Alrifi designs the decoration of mosques as part of his work. Next to the mosque is a tower, called a minaret, from which the people are called to prayer. But before praying a Muslim must purify himself by the symbolic washing of his hands and feet. There is a fountain for this purpose in the courtyard.

We leave the *souq* to make our way back to the hotel. Manama also contains most of the ministries and government offices, although the ruling Emir lives in West Rifaa, another of the new towns. Sheikhs of the Al-Khalifa family have ruled Bahrain since 1783 – with occasional intervention from the British.

A store displaying traditional Arab jewelry, including necklaces, bracelets and anklets.

A fish stall in the market in Manama.

13

We meet the Al-Alrifi family

The next day our chauffeur takes us to the new town outside Manama where the Al-Alrifi family live. We travel through the outskirts of the town passing low, flat-roofed, white buildings set in date palm groves. Finally, we find ourselves speeding along the dusty road through the countryside.

The northern area of the island has been irrigated and cultivated. There are orchards of banana, citrus, mango and pomegranate trees as well as groves of date palms. A few cattle graze, and some vegetables are grown in the shade of the trees.

This area is very different from the dry, sandy plains of the southern part where few people live permanently. The fishermen who live there make their houses out of *barasti*, the canes from date palms.

Ahmed and Kawkab Al-Alrifi and their two children, Maryam, age 4, and Hathem, age 3, greet us warmly outside their bungalow. Ahmed and Hathem are wearing traditional dress. Arab men wear long, white, billowy robes so that they can keep cool in the extreme heat. The headdress is called a *haik*. It consists of a piece of cloth held in place with a cord around the crown of the head.

The new town they live in was designed so that everything a family might need would be close by. The Al-Alrifi's home is near a supermarket, a modern kindergarten, a good library and a mosque.

Ahmed and Kawkab lead us into the house, which consists of five big rooms with a kitchen and bathroom. Like many modern houses in Bahrain, it is air-conditioned.

We sit in the living room, which is also Ahmed's work room. It has a magnificent, thick Persian rug on the floor. Ahmed brings us some very strong, black, bitter coffee. Drinking alcohol is forbidden by Islam and so coffee is the favorite social drink. In the *souqs* there are coffee houses where men meet to talk and to enjoy smoking a hubble-bubble pipe.

The Al-Alrifi family stand outside their home. They rent the house from the state.

15

Ahmed Al-Alrifi

Ahmed, who is 36 years old, studied interior design in Cairo, Egypt, for five years. Since 1971, when he finished his studies, he has been working for the government in the Arts Ministry.

"I arrange art exhibitions, give grants and try to help local artists come forward with their art," Ahmed tells us. He is a practicing artist himself. He designs decoration for houses and mosques and produces large sculptures for public parks and gardens.

"It was the teachers at school who said

Ahmed is an artist and works for the government. In his spare time he likes to go fishing.

that I should be an artist. My father had nothing against it, although he wasn't too happy that I should do portraits. He is very religious and this would not be acceptable within the teachings of the Koran." Ahmed explains, "The Koran is the sacred book of Islam. It is believed to contain the actual words spoken by Allah – which is the Muslim name for God – to the Angel Gabriel, which he then revealed to Mohammed. It is a complete guide to life for Muslims."

He went on, "I was the youngest in our family with three brothers and six sisters. The Koran was the basis of our education. Through it I learned to love my parents and to respect others. I also learned that Allah watches over me whatever I may do, right or wrong."

Ahmed is a collector. "I like old and beautiful things; that's why I collect them," Ahmed says, taking some seals from the shelves in the dining room where he keeps his collection. "These are from Bahrain and are 400 years old. Bahrain was an important trading center at that time."

Ahmed is working on a piece of decoration for the outside of a house.

Ahmed will give Maryam a good education.

Ahmed also likes fishing and in the winter he often goes south with many of his friends to fish off the coast. They set up camp between the beach and the desert. They stay for a week or more, cooking their food in the open and playing music.

"Sometimes all our families come as well but, more often, the men go on their own," he says. "Fishing used to be an important industry in Bahrain. Many fishermen now find they can earn more money ashore. Building dhows and diving for pearls were important too. But now these exist on a very small scale because there is less of a demand and large quantities of pearls are cultured artificially in Japan and the Far East."

A group of weavers show Ahmed their work.

Kawkab Al-Alrifi

Kawkab, who is 26 years old, works part-time in the Housing Ministry and reads a lot in her spare time. She studied sociology and psychology for four years.

"It's thanks to oil that there has been such an enormous improvement in lifestyle during the past ten years. We can buy more varied and better goods in the stores, for example. Housing has improved too. This year alone over a thousand new homes have been built.

Kawkab thinks that everybody's lifestyle has improved since the discovery of oil.

They are allocated to families in June and December according to the reports which I make," she explains.

"When a family has sent an application for a new house, I go and visit them. I make a report on the size of the family, where they are living now, how far they have to travel to work, and other things like that." She goes on, "The rents are about 87 Bahrain dinar a month, but if a family has a higher income they pay more. In the same way, really poor families pay nothing. Houses rented from the state become the property of the tenant after twenty-five years."

"Besides these much needed improvements, there are more educational opportunities, particularly for women," she says. We ask her how she and Ahmed met. "My brother and Ahmed are friends, so when I was looking for a job in the Ministry he sent me to see Ahmed. There were no vacancies at the time but Ahmed promised to find me one if he could. We quickly got to know each other and then we married a few years ago," she says, smiling.

Kawkab is in her office at the Housing Ministry, where she works on a new housing project.

A Muslim upbringing

Maryam is wearing the traditional Arab headdress inlaid with gold.

Ahmed and Kawkab play an equal part in bringing up their children. They have very strong views about how it should be done.

"It is most important for us that the children be happy. They will both have a good education, which is free here in Bahrain. We will let them develop at their own pace and will not push them," Ahmed says. "The children have to learn for themselves how to do things. I tell them when they do things right or wrong," he adds.

We asked Kawkab about her own childhood. "My parents were very strict. When I was a child, children weren't allowed to be present when there were

Kawkab is very careful about the friends the children make, in case any are a bad influence.

guests. But times have changed in every way. We certainly move with the times but I'm still very careful about the friends they make, in case there are any who may be a bad influence. Perhaps you think I'm over-protective," she says, laughing.

Kawkab is very religious and prays five times a day. During Ramadan she keeps to the times of fasting and she neve. drinks alcohol. She explains, "Ramadan is the ninth month of the Muslim year and it is a month of fasting. The Islamic year is based on lunar months and is shorter than the Western one. During Ramadan, eating, drinking and smoking are forbidden between sunrise and sunset. At the end of the month each family has a feast to celebrate.

The children wait to say goodnight to their parents.

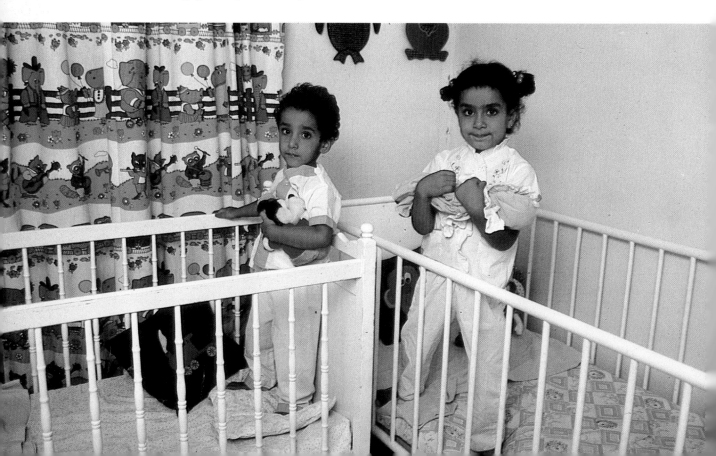

Kawkab continues, "If I don't pray just before I go to bed, then I can't fall asleep. Religion means a lot to me, and I keep closely to the teachings of the Koran. I want to make the pilgrimage to Mecca, which is the holiest place of Islam. The pilgrimage is known as the *hadj* and happens once a year. Thousands of people come from all over the world. All Muslims are expected to do this at least once in their lives."

Ahmed is not as religious, but just like Kawkab he will make sure that the children are.

We talk about what they would look for in their future son-in-law. The choice of husband for Maryam will be very important. "It doesn't matter so much if he is rich or poor. He should be responsible with firm religious beliefs, and preferably be as well educated as my daughter." Kawkab adds, "If we don't accept him as a son-in-law then my daughter can't marry him."

Maryam will marry when she is about 20 years old and in the Arab tradition she will have a collection of special clothes, including gold-inlaid dresses. She will also have head jewelry, necklaces, bracelets and rings.

Kawkab and Maryam wear the same traditional style of dress, decorated with gold stitching.

25

Family life

Kawkab is at work in the mornings between 7 a.m. and 1 p.m. Ahmed also works during these hours while Maryam goes to the kindergarten nearby. Maryam really enjoys going to kindergarten where she draws and paints and plays with the other children. She also watches school programs on television and video.

Ahmed and Kawkab employ a young girl to help in the house, so that Kawkab does not do all the housework. "I still do most of the cooking, but that's because I enjoy it so much," she says. She also helps look after Hathem, who is very shy. Soon he will be going to kindergarten with his sister.

In the evenings, once they have eaten and the children have been put to bed, Ahmed and Kawkab relax by watching television. "There are very many programs worth watching. Many good foreign programs are shown," Ahmed tells us. "This is another sign of the general progress that is being made here."

Maryam enjoys going to the kindergarten and playing with the other children.

Ahmed and Kawkab relax by watching television, when the children have gone to bed.

Mealtime

Kawkab does most of the cooking because she enjoys it so much.

Kawkab prepares for us a delicious meal of *makbose*. This is the family's favorite dish, which is a mixture of fish, rice, tomatoes, onions, and spices. The fish they use is called *hamoor*, which is found in Bahrain. Kawkab tells us, "We always eat crabs as well with *makbose*. They are boiled in a little water with lemon powder and salt. We make our own bread from a stiff dough which is rolled out into a pancake. This is then baked at a high temperature, in a special cylinder-shaped oven."

Over the coffee that follows the meal we ask them what they see for their future in Bahrain.

"We think the future looks bright. We believe that the progress that has been made in education, the social services, transportation and communications will go on, and improve the lives of many more people," Ahmed says. Kawkab adds, "We hope that our family will remain close and just as we look after Ahmed's mother, our children will take care of us when we get old."

It is getting late and time for us to catch our bus back to Manama. We thank Ahmed and Kawkab for spending such an interesting and enjoyable day with us.

Makbose – *the family's favorite dish. Crabs are often eaten with it.*

Facts about the Middle East

Bahrain

Size: 669.26 sq. km. (260 sq. mi.). **Capital city:** Manama. **Population:** 350,700

Iran

Size: 1,600,000 sq. km. (617,760 sq. mi.). **Capital city:** Tehran. **Population:** 35 million

Iraq

Size: 438,446 sq. km. (171,267 sq. mi.). **Capital city:** Baghdad. **Population:** 13.53 million

Kuwait

Size: 17,818 sq. km. (6,879 sq. mi.) **Capital city:** Kuwait City. **Population:** 1.25 million

Oman

Size: 212,380 sq. km. (82,000 sq. mi.). **Capital city:** Muscat. **Population:** 1.5 million

Qatar

Size: 10,360 sq. km. (4,000 sq. mi.). **Capital city:** Doha. **Population:** 200,000

Saudi Arabia

Size: 2,400,000 sq. km. (865,000 sq. mi.) **Capital city:** Riyadh. **Population:** 9 million

United Arab Emirates

Size: 83,650 sq. km. (32,300 sq. mi.). **Capital city:** Abu Dhabi. **Population:** 850,000

Language: Arabic is the main language of all the countries, except Iran where Persian is spoken.

Religion: The main religion in the Middle East is Islam.

Climate: Generally the climate is very hot and dry. Summer temperatures can be as high as 49°C (120°F); winter temperatures average 21°C (70°F). Rainfall is low – averaging between ½ inch to 3 inches (13mm–75mm) per year, except over the mountainous areas of Iran and Iraq.

Agriculture: New methods are always being experimented with, but still a relatively small proportion of land is irrigated and cultivated. Crops include vegetables, fruit, and cereals. Dairy farming is being developed.

Industry: Oil is the main source of industry. New industries are being developed for the time when oil reserves get low – for example, aluminum smelting, steel manufacture, ship repairs. Assembly plants are being set up for cars and domestic appliances.

Glossary

Archipelago A group of small islands.

Causeway A raised road across water or marshy ground.

Dhow A traditional wooden Arab boat.

Dome The rounded roof of a building.

Fasting To go without food and drink for a long period of time.

Grant A gift of money.

Hubble-bubble pipe A pipe for smoking tobacco through a container of water. The water cools the smoke.

Irrigation A means of bringing water to very dry areas of land, so that they can be cultivated.

Islam The main religion in the Middle East.

Kindergarten A school for very young children.

Koran The sacred book of Islam.

Muslim Someone who practices the religion of Islam.

Ramadan An Islamic month of fasting, when Muslims are not allowed to drink or eat between sunrise and sunset.

Souq An old market area of a Middle Eastern city. It consists of lots of narrow streets full of small stores.

Index

Acknowledgments

All the illustrations in this book were supplied by the authors, with the exception of the following:
John Topham (Bernard Gerard) 6; Camerapix Hutchison Library 8, 11; John Topham (Christine Osborne) 13. The maps on pages 7 and 9 were drawn by Bill Donohoe.